I relio
attract

Inner h
within me

I attract all that is meant for
my highest good

I welcome balance and harmony
within myself to enlighten
my relationships to myself and
others

I am whole

I now set the intention to create
the most magical day

I have the ability to attract
success, abundance and wealth
today

I am at peace

I believe

I am ready

Everyday I am the happiest,
hottest, healthiest and
richest version of myself
The love I give to others
is reflected back to me and
the Universe is always working
in my favour.

LightTools

GRATITUDE JOURNAL

BY

JOANNA HUNTER

www.joannahunter.com

@joannahuntercom

The information in this book/journal should not be used as a substitute for medical or mental health advice. Always consult a medical or mental health practitioner when in need. The intent of the author is only to offer information of a general nature to help you create actionable steps, clarity, and momentum in your goals for the future. In the event you use any of the information in this book/journal for yourself, the author and publisher assume no responsibility or liability for your actions.

ISBN **978-0-9933027-4-9**

First Edition 2017 - **Paperback**

Authored by Joanna Hunter

Cover design & Formatting by Paul Hunter

Published by My Inner Peace Publishing

DEDICATION

To anyone who has ever felt there has got to be more to life, let this gratitude journal create that pathway to more.

LightTools

TABLE OF CONTENTS

ONE POSITIVE THOUGHT IN THE MORNING CAN CHANGE MY WHOLE DAY!

FOREWORD

This is a two-in-one LightTool™. We have combined the power of gratitude journalling with some amazing affirmations to help you bring more light into your life.

It is my heartfelt hope that this journal is the answer for everyone who has ever been caught in the ego trap and said the words, "I will be happy when, __________." Fill in the blank of your choice.

We think when we have the car of our dreams, the life partner we want, the big house, the job we desire, making the money we only once dreamed off, the skinny body, the super cute pool guy.... I could go on but you get the idea, we will be finally happy. Here's the simple straight up truth, you won't be happier, not even close.

Here's why; Happiness is a feeling not a thing. When we are happy, we are grateful. Happiness creates the feeling of gratitude.

I once had the law of attraction teacher Babel Mohr say to me;

"Joanna if you can't be grateful for what you have, what makes you think you will be happier with more?"

That question changed my life. It hit me over the head like a two by four first, but it changed my life! I thought a semblance of happiness lay in having more things.

IT'S OKAY
FOR ME
TO HAVE
EVERYTHING
I DESIRE

So, I filled my life with what the magazines told me I should have, with all the stuff I once wanted because I believed my lack of happiness was a lack of something physical. In the moment of hearing that question, I realised I did not have lack, but I did have a lack of gratitude.

You see happiness is an intangible thing, a smile from a baby, a random act of kindness from stranger, a hug between two people at an airport that makes you believe in love, the sun on your face, a joke shared with good friends.

All those things can and will make us happy. Why? because all of those things bring us into the present moment where our true power lies. All too often our thoughts hang out in places where we are powerless, in the past making us depressed as it has already happened so we have no power there, or in the future making us anxious because it has not happened yet, so again there is no power there for us to draw on. Only the present moment has that power to connect us to Source.

Gratitude connects us to the present moment and the more we can connect to the now, the happier we become and the more present we become in our lives. It's time to get present and accounted for to live the life we dreamed of.

"Gratitude is the key"

I AM
A RIVER
OF GRATITUDE

WHY GIVE GRATITUDE?

What if there was a magic sauce that made everything in your life taste better, would you want it? This magic sauce was so brilliant it could cover the taste of life's most bitter experiences, even the ones of the past. What's more, this magic sauce is like my youngest child's definition of ketchup: it would make everything taste great and most certainly could be served with everything, even cornflakes! It could even guarantee that future experiences all tasted good naturally; would you want that magic sauce?

If you are in your adult life you probably have lost count of the number of times you have heard this tiny statement: "count your blessings". Just because you have heard something often does not make it any less meaningful or powerful!

I must have heard 'count your blessings' a million times before I fully understood what it really meant, or how it would truly benefit me. We live in a universe where what you give attention to expands. Please read this statement again: what you give attention to expands! Since thinking about our worries is at epidemic proportions within the human population, it is little wonder that our worries can show up over and over again as the negative experiences of our lives since what we give attention to expands.

We are going to change all that- oh YES we are!

What's more, it's simple! Really, really - freaking - simple - a two year old could do it! It will change your life! I get soooo

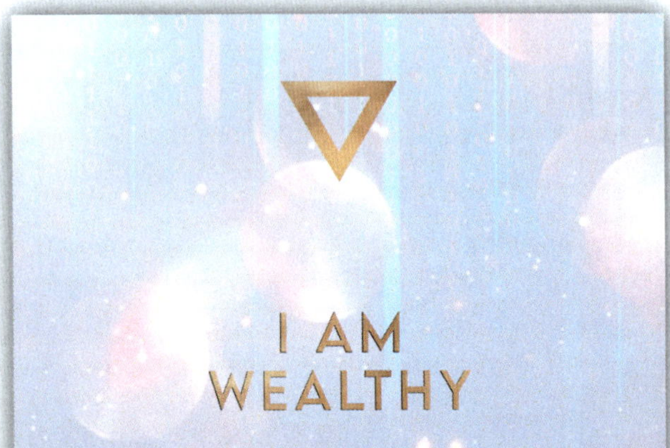
I AM
WEALTHY

excited to tell people about this as it totally changed my life in such wondrous ways that, even though I have practiced this for 12 plus years, I am still awed by it. As a beautiful bonus, I have had the total privilege to witness hundreds of people's lives transformed as a result of teaching this simple practice - Ya-aay - for magic sauce!

Talking of magic: Imagine if I were to put my fairy godmother wings on, break out my magic wand (because you know I totally own one) and grant you your heart's dearest desires - anything you like! (pretend fairy godmother me is generous like that). Then, a whole lotta glitter, sparkles and twinkly bells later (because that's how my inner fairy godmother rolls)...Ta-dah! Your heart's desire is now yours;. On a scale of one to ten how grateful would you be?

All jesting aside, that little question is actually really important. If your answer was something like, "Are you kidding me? I'd be so grateful," it tells us something hugely significant about your heart's dearest desires. That is; your heart's dearest desires live at the vibration of gratitude. If you read my book "Get Selfish - The Way Is Through", you might recall the Albert Einstein quote in the chapter entitled the Law of Manifestation. If not, here it is:

"Everything is energy and that's all there is to it. Match the frequency of the reality you want and you will get that reality. There can be no other way. This is not Philosophy. This is physics."

That is the essence of keeping a 'Gratitude Journal'. We are consciously going to shift our thoughts to a more grateful

I HAVE A
MILLIONAIRE
MINDSET

'frequency' or vibration, since what we give our attention to expands. This will powerfully expand the energy of our heart's dearest desires within our lives and give us more of our heart's dearest desires. It's the 'magic sauce' that will powerfully make life taste soooo much better than perhaps what you are currently experiencing. In this Journal I am going to give you my best tips for making gratitude a daily part of your life, as well as share with you some powerful life transforming affirmations.

Here's a practical tip for when to do your gratitude journal - now it's important for me to say that there are no hard and fast rules on when you do it - obviously it's better to do your gratitude journal than not at all, but if you can't manage this tip don't sweat it.

I find writing at least ten gratitudes down each evening before I go to bed is a really effective way to use a gratitude journal, that way my last thoughts for the day are of gratitude. Then I add in the practice of reading them every morning and allowing myself to really feel the feeling of gratitude for each of those entries first thing.

Very quickly my days become 'sandwiched' between my gratitude practices so it becomes easier for the bit in the middle to be positive too.

ALL THAT I
DESIRE IS
ALREADY
WITHIN ME

GIVING

'It is in the giving we receive': another chestnut of wisdom from our human collective. Like 'Count your blessings,' I've heard this one said many times also, and it is so true. However, I didn't fully appreciate the truth in this little statement until I understood the universe was responding to me through the virtue of my thoughts.

Since the universe multiplies what you give out, and mirrors it back to you, in effect 'You reap what you sow': I could not miss the opportunity to exult the virtues of giving.

Giving is a tricky subject as we have to give from the right base of energy in order for it to work to our benefit. You might think you know people who give all the time buuuut they seem no better off for it. It might even be you who gives all the time with no particular reward. Here's where it gets tricky; the best type of giving is done from an open and grateful heart with no thought to our own benefit at all, and only to the benefit of the person we are giving too. Often life's givers give from an energy base of sacrifice, since sacrifice implies scarcity. The energy base is one of not enough and therefore that is what is reflected back; not enough.

When we give from an open and grateful heart this allows the energy to be as pure and high vibrational as possible. The high vibrational energy we give out then becomes the energy which is mirrored back into our lives as experiences. That high vibration energy is the good stuff and also the energy

I
RADIATE
LOVE

where your own heart's desires live. Since we just gave all that juicy attention to it, it has to expand.

Whatever you want in life can be mirrored back to you and the easiest way to achieve this, apart from giving gratitude, is to give that which you desire. For example; you want the love of your life to show up in your life. You have been on a mission to seek them out for a long time but to no avail.

First you must be willing to become the love of your life by giving yourself self-love. Not only will this help you to attract love in, by placing you on the vibration of it, but will also allow you to accept that love once it arrives. This is paramount in keeping that love when it arrives in your life.

The second step is to give love to others in our daily lives. The universe gives what I like to think of as 'bonus points' to those who are able to love the people they have judged as undeserving of their love. You know, all those annoying people that get on your last nerve, the ones that somehow manage to push all of your buttons with amazing accuracy. If you can find love for them and see them with compassion, the universe mirrors the energy back to you in the form of love and inner peace. That is spiritual alchemy; thus your own situation must transform.

If you are trying to attract in money, begin to give of what you have, making sure when you do so you do it from an empowered, abundant state of energy with an open grateful and heart. DO NOT DO IT if you are begrudgingly giving every penny as it will only create more lack. In order for this to work, you need to get on the vibration of gratitude,

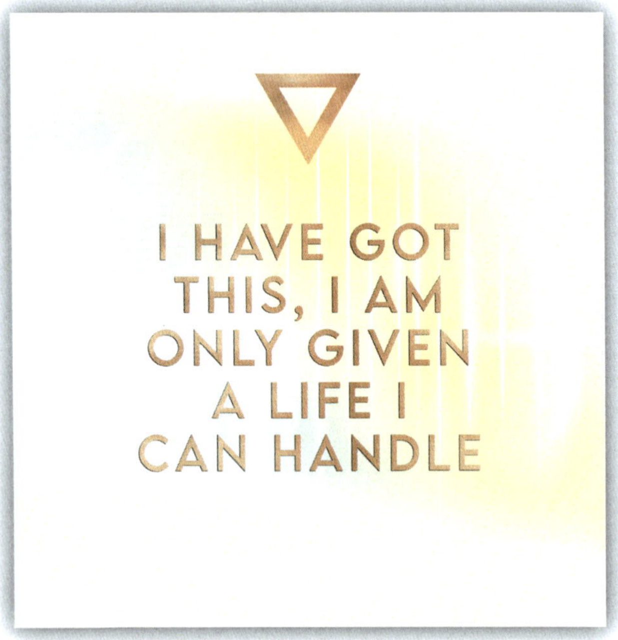
I HAVE GOT
THIS, I AM
ONLY GIVEN
A LIFE I
CAN HANDLE

give gratefully from that energy base. Also give praise and blessings to the money you already have, even if it is just pennies. If you are thinking about your lack, or how you are sacrificing the last of the money you have, you are operating from the energy of 'lack of' and will only attract back in a lack. If you give from gratitude you will expand your money.

When I am looking for something to come into my life, it doesn't matter what it is, I look to give it. If I am needing training in a certain area but have no teacher, I become the teacher for others and help them gain the knowledge they are seeking. In doing so I focus on how good it must feel for them to get answers they may have been seeking and allow their joy to become mine too. Sometimes the answers that I sought come from the teaching I give and other times a teacher will randomly appear and come into my life through some unexpected way; either way the universe mirrored back to me that which I gave.

It works in a twofold way. By giving from an empowered mindset I am connecting to the abundance of the universe and disconnecting to my own inner lack or void. If you have read my book 'Get Selfish- The Way Is Through', you'll have a deeper understanding of the empowered state of being and how to get there.

By focusing on the joy that others may feel, I begin to feel good about myself and thus I once more connect to the abundant source within. Once I am on that vibration, simple physics takes over and that which I desire, which is on the same vibration, has to become my reality because like energy attracts like energy.

I AM CONSTANTLY EXPANDING INTO MY ABUNDANCE, JOY & HAPPINESS

AFFIRMATIONS

Affirmations are a powerful way to reprogram your mind with a new more positive program. In this book you will find some of my favourite affirmations for creating amazing shifts in your life.

They work by convincing our subconscious that they are true. Since we are also the creators of our reality they will become true when the energy/ attention we give them reaches a saturation point/critical mass. At this point they shift from the unseen (the non- physical world) into the seen (the physical world) and become our reality; kinda like a self-fulfilling prophecy- a good one!

How to use affirmations

If you are not really sure how to use affirmations, start by repeating them as many times as you can. A great tip is to do this when you are doing repetitive tasks or tasks where you don't have to think too much, like cleaning or when at the gym. Our brains are often very receptive when we do the mundane so adding an affirmation during these tasks will take advantage of this receptive state.

The game of liar ping pong

Now you might become aware of a game of liar ping pong starting to play out in your head. It goes like this: 'I am so healthy' you say and your mind pipes up 'Liar! You just ate cheese loaded nachos'. However the affirmation 'I am so

I ALWAYS
HAVE MORE
THAN
ENOUGH

'healthy' is actually the reality you want. So now, as I see it, you have three options:-

Option one - Cry into your nachos and order the thick shake because you are doomed to become a health failure!

Option two - You realise you are the creator of your reality and you will be having that healthy reality thank you very much, despite the nacho you just ate. So you keep going with, 'I am so healthy', knowing that the negative voice is also the weaker voice inside you, and you will eventually silence it as it is inherently lazy and will give up; that is its nature.

Option three - Outsmart the negative voice by only saying statements that are true. Instead of 'I am so healthy' where you might encounter resistance, use 'I love feeling healthy'. Just try it. Can you feel the difference in energy? No resistance, right? Because what you said was true.

So don't be afraid to modify the affirmations to suit yourself as the universe gives us more of what we give attention to. Focusing on 'healthy', especially with the feeling and energy of love, will increase it in your life. 'I love' - followed by the statement you want to be true is a great 'hack' for affirmations, because you are less likely to encounter your own resistance. Less resistance equals faster results.

Two ways I love to use affirmations:

Heart centred way: I say the affirmation then imagine it in my heart radiating out. I place my hands over my heart and

TODAY I
CHOOSE TO
REMEMBER I
AM INFINITE

breathe in the affirmation; I really imagine the statement is true. This creates a powerful shift within me that I wrap my energy in.

The affirmation shower: I say the affirmation, repeating it again and again as I imagine the words like a shower of source energy; bright golden-white light coming through my head/crown chakra permeating every cell of my body, adjusting, correcting and loving the cells into the frequency of my affirmation, powerfully shifting my frequency to emit this new frequency. The shower is cleansing away the old energy, and filling my cells with the new affirmation. As I do this I imagine the affirmation to be soooooo true and what my life would be like in this new reality.

After doing this I always feel different and more aligned to the affirmation.

Feel free to make your own affirmations, but be mindful of only giving attention to that which you want more of. So in that spirit understand 'I want to be debt free' does not make a good affirmation. The intention of the affirmation is good, however the wording will leave you in debt. As debt is a non-negotiable word it has one meaning and one meaning only; it means you owe something. If you focus on it, you will bring more of it to you

A better affirmation would be 'I love having financial freedom.' This statement will bring you the energy of financial freedom, which is ultimately what is desired in this scenario.

I CAN
&
I WILL

Here are a few other examples of better ways to word your affirmations for greater success.

I am pain free → I love how my body moves with ease & joy

I am losing weight → I am my perfect size & shape

I am never late → I am always on time

The key to affirmations working is to use them regularly and to be consistent. I have had many people tell me affirmations don't work, but upon further investigation I discover that, if they don't become skinny or wealthy in thirty six or so hours, they stopped using them!

So I will leave you with the immortal words of Zig Ziglar as this quote works for affirmations too!

"Positive thinking is like bathing; for it to be most effective, we recommend you do it daily"
-Zig Ziglar

If you would like further help using affirmations or learning other LightTools™ to change your life then check out my website - www.joannahunter.com

I AM
A BEING
OF UNLIMITED
SOURCE
ENERGY

April 4, 2000

DATE:

God, I am opening available for another couple of clients Thank-you! very much.

Thank-you so very much that my social media ads are bringing in more clients.

I am so blessed and grateful now that I have that loving committed relationship

I am so blessed and grateful now that I have that $2,000,000.00 to invest for my future.

I am so blessed and grateful for my beautiful home on the water

I am so blessed and grateful for my Honda Passport which provides me safety & stability on my trips

I am so blessed and grateful for my health

I am so blessed and grateful for my loving sons & family!

I ALLOW
MYSELF TO
SEE THE
BEAUTY IN
EVERYTHING

April 5, 2022

DATE:

I am so blessed & grateful for my bed

I am so blessed & grateful for my running water

I am so blessed & grateful for my health

I am so blessed & grateful for electricity

I am so blessed & grateful for everything in my home

I am so blessed & grateful for privacy at my home

I am so blessed & grateful for my eyesight that is excellent

I am so blessed & grateful for the food to nourish my body

I am so blessed & grateful for my appliances

I am so blessed & grateful for the sunshine

I
LOVE
BEING
ABUNDANT

April 6, 2023

DATE:

I am so blessed · grateful for

my great hearing.

I am so blessed · grateful for

my body

I am so blessed · grateful for.

Money.

I am so blessed · grateful for

my music.

A
RIVER OF
COMPASSION
RUNS THROUGH
ME
- RUMI

DATE:

EVERYTHING
IS ALWAYS
WORKING OUT
FOR ME

DATE:

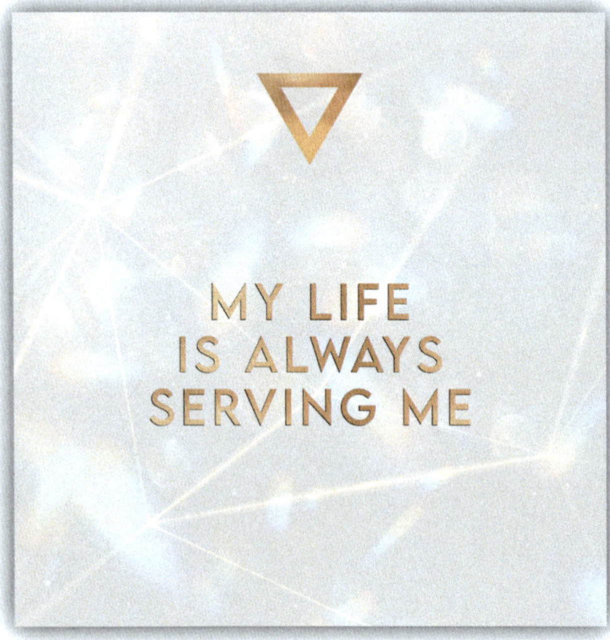
MY LIFE
IS ALWAYS
SERVING ME

DATE:

I
AM
LIMITLESS

DATE:

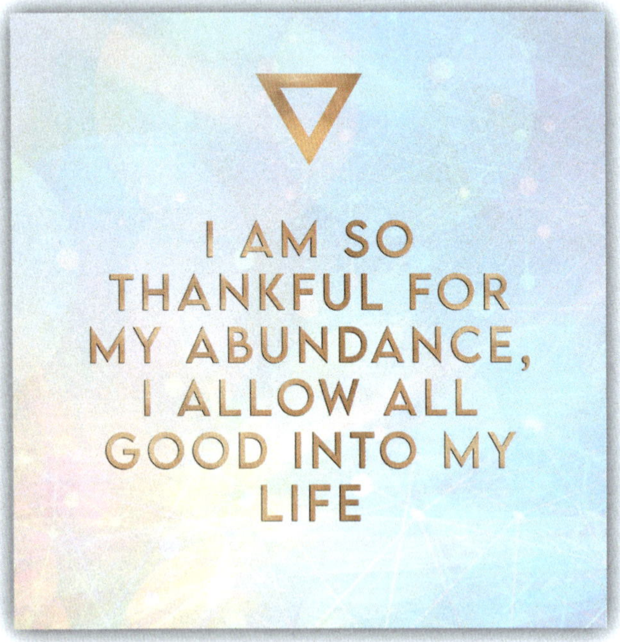
I AM SO
THANKFUL FOR
MY ABUNDANCE,
I ALLOW ALL
GOOD INTO MY
LIFE

DATE:

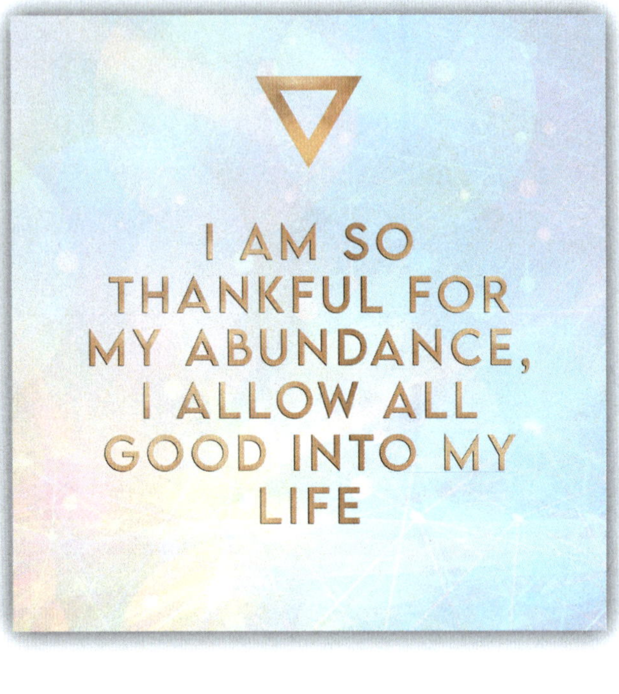
I AM SO
THANKFUL FOR
MY ABUNDANCE,
I ALLOW ALL
GOOD INTO MY
LIFE

DATE:

I
LOVE
BEING
HEALTHY

DATE:

MY
SOUL
ALWAYS
GUIDES ME
TO THE TRUTH!

DATE:

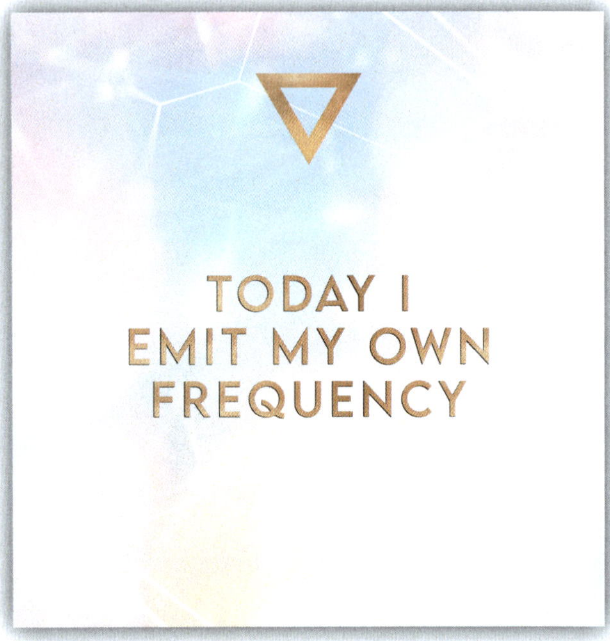
TODAY I
EMIT MY OWN
FREQUENCY

DATE:

I
HAVE ALL
THAT I NEED
FOR RIGHT
NOW!

DATE:

I
LOVE
FEELING
GORGEOUS!

DATE:

I AM
POWERFUL
BEYOND
MEASURE!

DATE:

EACH AND EVERY DAY MY RELATIONSHIPS JUST GET STRONGER AND MORE SUPPORTIVE OF ME!

DATE:

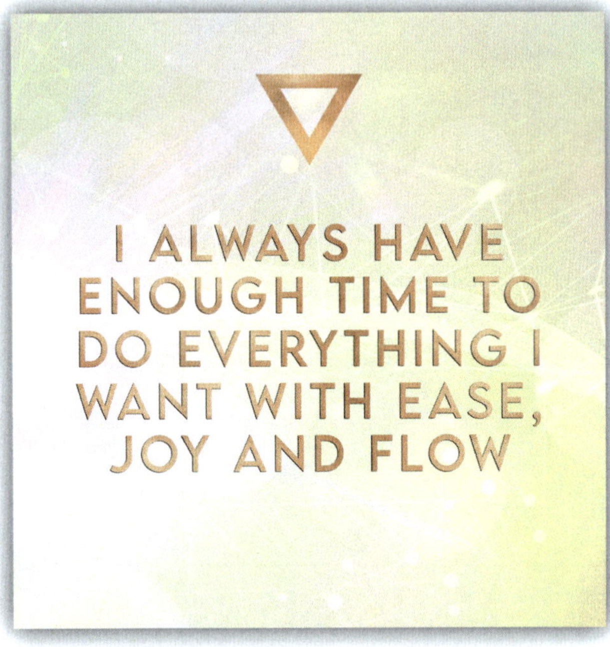
I ALWAYS HAVE
ENOUGH TIME TO
DO EVERYTHING I
WANT WITH EASE,
JOY AND FLOW

DATE:

MY EFFORTS
& LIFE ARE
ALWAYS
SUPPORTED BY
THE UNIVERSE

DATE:

I
AM
KIND

DATE:

MY LIFE IS
ALWAYS
SUPPORTING ME

DATE:

ALL
IS WELL
IN MY
WORLD

DATE:

I LOVE FEELING
COURAGEOUS &
I CHOOSE TO
STAND UP FOR
MYSELF!

DATE:

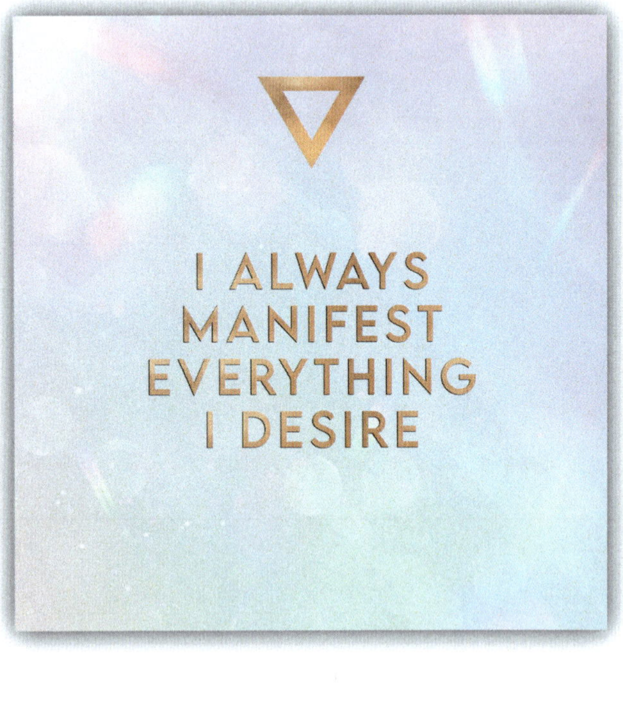
I ALWAYS
MANIFEST
EVERYTHING
I DESIRE

DATE:

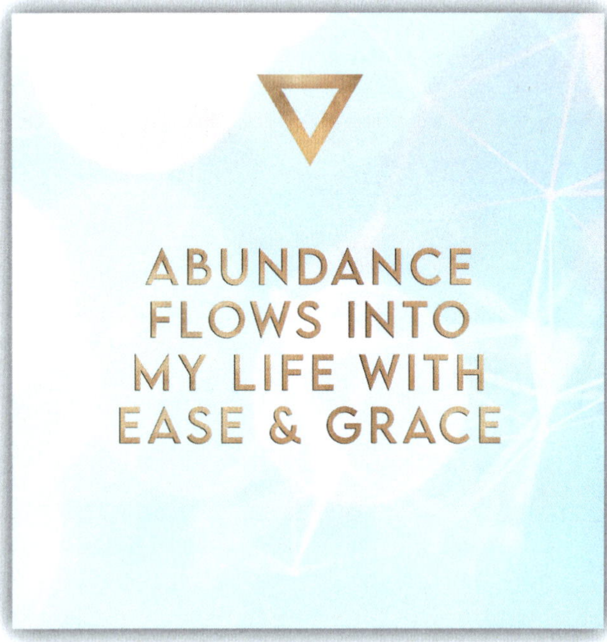
ABUNDANCE
FLOWS INTO
MY LIFE WITH
EASE & GRACE

DATE:

I
GET PAID
FOR BEING ME

DATE:

MY
POTENTIAL
TO SUCCEED
IS INFINITE

DATE:

I
AM A
MIRACLE

DATE:

I AM
AT PEACE

DATE:

TODAY I WILL
RESONATE
AT PEACE

DATE:

THE
UNIVERSE
GUIDES ME
EVERY STEP
OF THE WAY

DATE:

I
WRAP
MYSELF IN
MY OWN
LOVE

DATE:

I TRUST
MYSELF
WHOLLY AND
COMPLETELY

DATE:

I CHOOSE TO
FILL MY DAYS
WITH EASE,
JOY AND FLOW

DATE:

I AM A MAGNET FOR MONEY - MONEY FLOWS TO ME IN EVER INCREASING AMOUNTS

DATE:

TODAY
I INVITE
JOY INTO
MY LIFE

DATE:

I AM
WORTHY OF
MY DREAMS

DATE:

I
AM
ENOUGH

DATE:

I CHOOSE
TO MAKE THE
REST OF MY
LIFE, THE BEST
OF MY LIFE
- LOUISE L HAY

DATE:

TODAY I WILL BE
IN COMPLETE
ALIGNMENT
TO THE BEST
VERSION OF ME

DATE:

I AM
WORTHY
OF ALL
GOOD THINGS!

DATE:

I
TRUST
MY INNER
WISDOM

DATE:

I AM
OPEN TO
RECEIVING
WONDERFUL
OPPORTUNITIES

DATE:

MY GRATEFUL
HEART IS A
MAGNET FOR
MIRACLES

DATE:

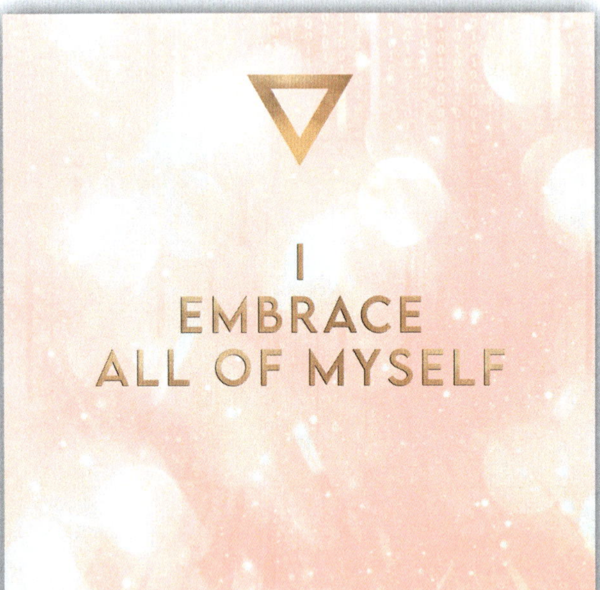
I
EMBRACE
ALL OF MYSELF

DATE:

EACH DAY I GET
BETTER & BETTER,
STRONGER &
STRONGER, MORE
COURAGEOUS &
CONFIDENT

DATE:

I HAVE THE
STRENGTH I NEED
TO FORGIVE
THOSE THAT NEED
IT, INCLUDING
MYSELF

DATE:

I LOVE
&
APPROVE
OF MYSELF

DATE:

I LOVE BEING
IN ALIGNMENT
WITH THE BEST
VESION OF ME

DATE:

I AM
READY TO
RECEIVE
ALL GOOD
NOW

DATE:

ALL THE
ANSWERS
I SEEK FLOW
TO ME
EFFORTLESSLY

DATE:

EVERY DAY
IS AN
OPPORTUNITY
FOR ME
TO SHINE

DATE:

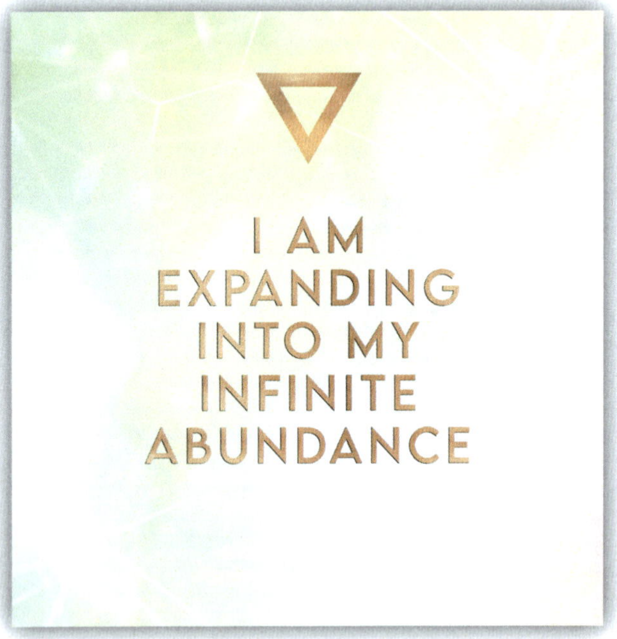
I AM
EXPANDING
INTO MY
INFINITE
ABUNDANCE

DATE:

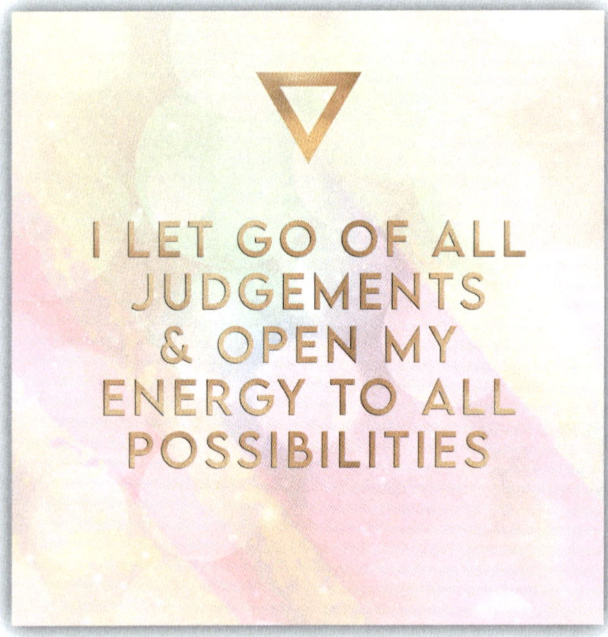
I LET GO OF ALL
JUDGEMENTS
& OPEN MY
ENERGY TO ALL
POSSIBILITIES

DATE:

EVERYTHING
CAN BE
FIGURED OUT

DATE:

HAPPINESS
IS MY
BIRTHRIGHT

DATE:

EVERYTHING
HAPPENS FOR
ME, EVERYTHING
IS ALWAYS
SUPPORTING ME

DATE:

EVERY CELL
IN MY BODY
SUPPORTS MY
HEALTH &
WELLNESS

DATE:

MY LOVE,
ENERGY AND
HAPPINESS
ARE LIMITLESS
& SO AM I!

DATE:

I
CAN DO
ANYTHING
I PUT MY
MIND TO

DATE:

TODAY,
WONDERFUL
THINGS WILL
UNFOLD FOR ME

DATE:

THIS IS MY TIME
& I AM READY
FOR THE NEXT
STEP

- DENISE DUFFIELD THOMAS

DATE:

I AM A
MONEY MAGNET

DATE:

I NOURISH MY
BODY, MIND &
SOUL WITH
SELF-LOVE

DATE:

I LOVE
&
ACCEPT MYSELF

DATE:

THANK YOU

ACKNOWLEDGMENTS

What is a gratitude journal without a lot of Thanks? I want to give deep, heartfelt thanks to the following people whose help has been invaluable in getting this project off the ground and into your hands dear reader. I want to thank you spirit team Skylar who are an ever present source of grace in my life, a reminder that we are all source energy and one. HUGE massive thanks to my clients who inspire me daily with their courage to change and their desire to become better versions of themselves. You have dared to believe in better and it's awe -inspiring to have been invited to be your guide, share part of your journey and be witness to your transformations.

I want to thank my amazing husband Paul who, many moons ago, learnt Indesign and Photoshop just because he has a 'crazy' wife who has a tonne of dreams and goals. He not only formatted this book and my other books but helped to design the cover. All of these skills he learnt so he could support me in making the world a happier place. I want to thank Team Hunter for their incredible support in our business and life, because sometimes it takes a village and mine is the best. I want to also thank my kids, Daniel, Ellen and Katie for their patience, love and humour, and as a source of constant inspiration in my life. My friends thank you for providing such inspiration and insights on and offline. Keep being awesome.

Finally, I want to give a deep 'in my bones' thank you, to the practice of gratitude for coming into my life and changing my life the way it did. There is not a day that goes by where I don't feel grateful for this practice, as it has so powerfully aligned my life with more things to be grateful for and has created happiness for me in the NOW.

A GRATEFUL HEART OPENS ALL DOORS

ABOUT JOANNA HUNTER

Joanna was born in Stockholm, Sweden. She moved to the magical Highlands of Scotland where she now lives with her husband, children and a nutty Jack Russell called Daisy. Joanna's calling has always been spiritual in nature, she was born with her spiritual gifts switched on. Joanna spends her days as a Spiritual Thought Leader, Author, Intuitive Spiritual Life and Business Coach, Law of Attraction Expert and High Priestess of the LightWeb; a soul based technology that will change your life.

Joanna works in partnership with her guides and spirit team, Skylar, a collective consciousness Joanna channels. Together they help people transition from an asleep state of being into a fully awakened state of being.

For Joanna self enrichment is not only a way of life but a wonderful calling of her soul; to help others lead happier more fulfilled lives is a beautiful bonus. Joanna is the founder of joannahunter.com and the Woo Woo Academy, where she teaches her international client base a range of courses on life, money, happiness, spiritual business and source connection. Joanna is the spiritual leader of leaders for a new paradigm, teaching YOUnity consciousness and self mastery.

Joanna is also the author of the book "Get Selfish- The way is through," and other LightTool™ journals available on amazon.com as well as other online/offline retailers.

You can connect with Joanna on Facebook **www.facebook.com/joannahuntercom** or on her website **www.joannahunter.com**

Join the mailing list for positivity, spiritual life & business insights and much more: **www.joannahunter.com**

NOTES

NOTES

NOTES

NOTES

Mantra

I am no longer available to things & people that make you feel like shit!

Manufactured by Amazon.ca
Bolton, ON

33154728R00100